NINTH IOTA

IRENE KORONAS

NEWTON-LE-WILLOWS

Published in the United Kingdom in 2018
by The Knives Forks And Spoons Press,
51 Pipit Avenue,
Newton-le-Willows,
Merseyside,
WA12 9RG.

ISBN 978-1-912211-13-5

Acknowledgements:

Grateful acknowledgement is made to the editors of the following publications, in which poems in this volume first appeared, sometime in earlier versions:

Otoliths: "sipylus," "dienesis," "theus," "uranus," "eumaeus"
Stride: "centaurs," "grypes," "katasterismoi"
Taos Journal of International Poetry & Art: "eurynome," "oracles"
X-Peri: "hermes," "hesiod 2," "hesiod 3"

Cover Art: *ninth iota,* Mixed Media Painting Digitally Enhanced with Apps. Artwork Copyright © Irene Koronas, 2016

TABLE OF CONTENTS

NINTH IOTA

aphrodite bondage

drunk in vulgar
virgin genitals

red skin and rodite
split in half

the orgies cast
the trod

anemone dip

metahose breasts
in beard affection

Irene Koronas

agamemnon

murder fed to a vow
restores the rule

of generations

house atone
half human
half god

trojan war

tricks appease
the outsource kill

a horse drawn
from war

opines disaster
toys

death of pelias

infant permit
to grant blood and expire
dash brains
so small as to conceal
twelve disguises
serpent piety
she cut
into thirteen pieces
inside the lie
a torch
the ambush
the banish
omits the effete
with affect

eurynome

chaos found her talius
from balaam

she with child
brood coil

bruise her prime
sprang from bone

a cosmog bitch
on the deity list

vaux body
dorsal

Irene Koronas

oracles

clank
the priest on fumes

            killing together

entrails and bull blood
poison answers

and lodge genius
to anoint the legs

of dizzy oracles
in their own cult

hexameter
or double axe

            chew by the orgy
tholos
wrynecks
knuckle bone two by four
exact virginity
to consecrate

the mock death

castration of uranus

genital the sick furies
to avenge parricide

hand brothers

free
mini suppliants

with obsidian
from thighs

Irene Koronas

dethronement of cronus

to marry his sister
he swallows a child

dead cast
his thong
on her navel
her emetic mix

vomit the prim key
gorge and fire lunation

clear
cannibal

consort hymn
their mythography
overrun by siege

cognates worship

prescient to be real
has given

birth of athena

skin grief
by aegis

her bag mask
fringe

cowries cry
ololu
ololu

a third begot

Irene Koronas

birth of heracles

to return identity

to sell
a club of muscle

in a bastard home

yoke his mind
flick his cuckold

finger cross
by travail

turn her into a whore

over
his greek
hung the virile
chorus

atreus and thyestes

fratricide in refrain

she gives him
a primogeniture
to throw open

the vagine course

sold for nominal return
in error

hack limbs
boil in calindas

the seed of flee
throats a black
rescue into her tit

incestuous corpse
collects grammar
and dials interrex

Irene Koronas

birth of eros

swat without cum
make him shoot blanks

perverse and phallic
antic crease relief

hint at incestus
strong as target

hestia

offer ronus
a rival suit
crifice in token slot

the mestic hear
from phipus
her necdotal

or holy size and trance

oil paint
red white
and black

Irene Koronas

zagreus

phycal pierce
the conblem hymn
surrogate illus

totemistic

orphic devotees
leap gyps
tuft of murder

flesh banquet

short reat bolt
hurls chalky men
into the underworld

of mother repeats

afterworld

rimibitants to reincarnate

sepulchral bodies blur led

metempsychosis
            despite privilege

various apps from hell

                damn anubis
                damn tartarus

                        the tar infernal
                        coffin decay

her tribute
to tripartite guests is small

five ages

bore the girl
        labor drip

rant on resin
        pit genii

the fourth race argonauts
convicts like dogma
        are late creations

gaia

white aniconic charcoal
sprouts dead kings

full of crease
anal divinity

coition blood
flocks lunar after when

sipylus

drones of gods recoil
hung against the waste

in scoop and skull cracks
his stratagem
vicarious as father sin

in rack
revives raid
drawn from bare ignominy

his ascension a blade in history
sever the secondhand altar

converts the poise
to a metadisc
rich in fate

dienesis

putate
my meanour
my tumnal flea
my muscaria

induce phetic nergy

muscle ecosis
only a goad route

to berserk
a slender dung

panaeolus

break the swore
keep rank immort
trace no fermix

classic transrite

heaven and hell
gender language
treat them

to off talk
convert argos
to mouth

fresco to tissue

theus

obduracy the new crush
mocks abuse
from destruct

witness suffers
the other apathy
take grandeur

impress the ever since
eminent figure
fire and craft own much

the same epithance
in cunning prow

most form culinity
most sauvage theft
most procure to extreme

bout that hose portion
who mutilate the dark
deeds against

the pregnant point
in hide in bring
her guile
gorge

arouse
respect the deliverer
of prim

in peculiar
call
to singe

uranus

dig one low embrace
theogony spread full on her guise
conjugal in recur motif

play a persist
ere of precanter huge and comic
the tamer taste

bred in mythic gust

Irene Koronas

eumaeus

1

cut telemachus
incubate the footstool

killed by nurse
to toast the yank intent
from spun

she grips his bent string
leaks sacrosanct

the blood axiom
genitals cast to dogs

2

vigor truce to combine verdict
cross and fatal stings
the savage shame by coquetry

orgies turn matrilocal

for promiscuity
cheapens market and sutures
her greek epic dismember

trojan

horse errors
from water frieze
his worn bezel booty

fir plank trap fit
to consecrate
an absurd coax

the party camp
beacon stood
her citadel belly roll

stuck his quiver
wind with blood
fetters their vessels

stole her temple
flame a placatory gift
will ruin sound
invented by a bull

the priest
angered by celibacy
lying coil his crush

to convince
garland the mane
carpet its hooves

tremble head
trolls flank voice
over mouth

strangle the bark
dog blaze crept
from the city tomb

chips in cresset
in low voice
unlock his neck

mount his face
dart his curtain

death of achilles

in erinnyes
they purify hands
sever the dead by necrophilia

gouge out eyes
lust struck a drag enemy
to murder

carve shame traitors
against vain bone
beside the burn scales
of air circuits

divide the zodiac
lacerate the press
that bronze corpse
in agony

back to murder secret
until cenotaph in text
slurp the worship
the virile heel

selene

fashion to dismiss
the chimerical she

beast a corpus

shorthand graphic
and meme theogony

scatters aniconic
and crone clip

lemnians

invite a coin flip
novice brawl

the dead plead
with a loud force
and vacant itch

a revelry dock
a little pitch
on tier

placates carnage
an omen vessel
cast off

ion

delay the sanctuary
offering him poison

to taste divine descent
mistaken for pastoral use

to witchcraft him

leviathan

from a snarl
the scaly girl

drips with ash
noble and cruel

for hard boys
who despise sex

Irene Koronas

orpheus

the sound pattern
of beasts after a visit
to argonia

charmed by torture

his lost neglect
burst from limbs
thrown into rivers

to clean blood from name
to void rooted men

laid in prophesy
drift and decapitate on variants
double-axe facts

confined as fugitive graft
mimics the orphic curve

of trophies on every lap

ganymedes

disguise to insult her
hebe image
pours the new host

abduction
an equal

view
a mock thigh

his solar scent

interrex rule
snatched up fancy

dung kill

fertility temple

exploit

platonic breeders

stir fresh
catamite objects
from a flagon

of poor subjects

hade

uncle hades

some say his leap
is a clash of gypsum

enemies slept

knuckle in firm
torn grisly

short cartilage
collect and buried

in the cord
daub hymn

now canonic
did not reach

underground

a fifty-headed dog
twits

her consent

hounds the crones
with brass stud

held in prime fissures

stood noisy
an antirape smell of decay

in tripartite pangs

nemesis

this heap from horns
a ball to chance up and down

favored parts in one hand
crown with stag

hangs by her girdle
her last egg laid

dice and his half circle rival
fructify the chase

devour the v formation flight
an image rate should ash

oceanus

three gorgon lie
to decapitate medusa

grips her head
to skin rays

one tooth
half woman half serpent

snatch up wide
venom coils

the hebrew rahab
the babylonian tiamat

masks on strangers
spoils the bread

makes rites a stone chest

cut corpses
held by salt

Irene Koronas

revolt

an assault on numbers seize
and grope the loose revive
into posture

strangle lust
beat his retch
eyerib torch

red deal
blows apart braze
his apotheosis

a boner repulse
the farcical warts

then mimic
then counteract

flood

sodic anger floods
a wolf struck by lightning

mixes the guts of goats
sent by parnassus

the cold augury
renews language

mother anecdote
between cannibals

to slave invention
and suppress cult

red into sacral fuse

Irene Koronas

prometheus

chain a gap
to bull fortitude

buried in mud
to extirpate a man

jointed in fat choice
fire flesh on clay

his savage idle
spite lies from heliacal

detail stretching nets
invented for punishment

maims his right hand

eos and orion

mount her
until she seduces
a beg shrill

lock him into advent
into an erotic pelt
marriage claims

a rumor a skinfold satyr
an oracle socket
transfix her disguise

strung rituals
combat and reign
stolen from clumsy

wearing a tiara

Irene Koronas

hellen

to preclude
waves

poseidon fell on her
fisted sister

his fondle call

her gird reek
the sidereal breast

drags customers with white gloves
pole dancers crow cock

gonads reemerge knuckle taught
yoke him over scorched film

tutelage cults graft for moral kill
titles torn drawn by chaste

shut in an empty tomb
she stabs herself

brooms the hole

to raise storms
crouched in revelation

suckled by a shegoat
dead body myth

eaten by latin

minos

antikill leash
a millipede protest
desert of gossip
his decoction
in thicket stiff appease
plucks dominion
carves miserere
the token devil
links her slip

phyliss and carya

to fight a leak
after the crack of a temple
nine women hang pliny

gouge his thracian eyes

Irene Koronas

theseus

himself a victim
cast in wool

balls ingratiate
further into her mouth

effeminate as deception
confuses her lewd

bauble of respect
on three walls

thread from lintel
led to naxos

his toss
into her brass pot

demons cut his
ecclesiastic face

ninth iota

reassemble a grimoire
with corpse in mouth
and heifers of iota

log in koine
unit of jot
the rogue interger

violent in logic
until the law passes
out of human count

god particle
god atom
god grain
god mite
god speck
god tad
god trace
god shred
god scintilla

Irene Koronas

gargon

gag snake
slain by demi femme

laid with supra
bit sisters

fang and tusk
the apotropaic
is profane

long menis

change god into
a compendium

of idle wit
divert and list

course or doubt
in hard contrast

joint cavity

Irene Koronas

hybristica

retire the furies
compel to kill
without breasts
their savage shape
running it

troezen

his bastard theatre
jabs her horror

rapt in eye
tag cut

lock the prick
in a thick charm

prophet hand

vesper bride

Irene Koronas

centaurs

port
in each nubile

seat at a table
of ixion

from paranymph
found in battle

halters his hoof

tartarus

exculpate the loser
flesh lash and mutilation

hades sticking to cock

quake chain
the jaw monere

a transfer hero
subservient to lust

Irene Koronas

death of theseus

absent the raze
stadia an express god

spite with power
subject to obscure

safety pins
helter his lineage

a prandial argonaut
stalks extinction

in polished black

oedipus

blind into drift
a thick shrank

bruise flung
with one voice

devours spot
bloody from dash to pieces

licks ears
with crease
coupling the pin torment

a swollen incest
in error wince

the greek fabulist
blades the priest
buried in taboo

Irene Koronas

seven against thebes

agree to reign
his obey
knocks up the count

swore to revenge
inking doom

pleats his brain
to thrust impiety bolts
on cremation rite

epigoni

argive bribe
seer sack

stands an odd hand
a halt cover

shelters mad regard

silt dare her hard blab
and prank

shot up reruns
track virgins

in offence
of the delphic squeal

manticore

cinnabar eyes
tail its cubit end

sting inflicts distance

thick androphagos
devours human claws

spikes a shag
in a bulrush voice

omphale

incur for omniscient
trenches a lip off scoop

crack to crush
and closet the harpies

scullion flesh converts
poise to disk the slope

hot odes gait thighs
sequel bag for genitals

Irene Koronas

pelops

under mate
a skull axle

lynch
post with a kick
laid on corpse

murder and cenotaph
dances
on a mock circuit

madden by drugs
becoming
solar beasts

hecatombs hide
the phallus pieces
of an assgod

victrix

breasts
fixed by sack

tease bastards
struck

with the thugs
of black
tripods

apousia

absence
left to flesh

primogeniture
grim with dial

immutable
on point morsels

musk
the sideway kick

wrist bleed
by sharp retrograde

sexual adoption
surrogates chaste

kata timi

[against honor]

under arms she fled

the opposite snare
to overleap

his fence
prostrate to smite
gory ear

out drains the brute
foul art

pity absent
for burnt breasts

caught in refuse

ploutos

blind divinities
are back

lay open
their shouts

praise god eye
hate serve poor

uptight poltroon
pitch lust for hit

double origin
end dare
beg drivel

lick quick
tell me
wealth

bellerophontes

gullet beast
presume

etymology p.632
chimaera breaks

blaze raiment
by intent

held the savage
steed

panoply
bitter
from neck

aurae

nopin link
shim warn

or javascript
option

light kill

crag
stricken

orestes

embroidery
tutor

laymate
in ringlet

worship
hecatomb

his paramour
tack hood

pious sequel
bound by 0

Irene Koronas

himeros

a long
conchshell

mocks
nest sex

egg hatches
curl fragment 67

praxitele skin
lunge guile

hesiod

click
papyri

(begot)
overbold

cyprus 35° 10’ 0”N
33° 22’ 0” E

ankle ripe
(lacuna)

glisse

Irene Koronas

grypes

napkins
quarter bolt

knot
behind legs

eyes
on shoulders

hairy
skull fleck

mud slings
vanish

poseidon

fraxinus
chthonic quake

doric
in linear b

seraph
cave cult

heavy
with veins

screwfish
violate arcadia

landlock
helenes burst

seahags
masturbate

battle
over glass letters

lustral polis
in brine

Irene Koronas

katasterismoi

point
in pole

heliacal
dome

lilumu
hyperborean

rim
tartaros pit

beast
in underworld

devours
chain and rock

hyginus 2.11
aratus 197

horizontal
cheiron omen

artemis

follow
(*chiton*)
ortygia pelts

(hom. *Il.* vi. 205,
427, &c., xix.

59, xxi.
483, &c.; *Od.* xi.

172, &c.,
324, xv.

478, xviii.
202, xx. 61, &c., v.

in conjunction
(*Od.* xv. 410;
Il. xxiv. 606.)

Irene Koronas

chiliades

pactolus
    his lyric

  yoke
     prophets

     tribe cross
          libris

       twelve thousand
              sealed

choerilus

thespis
competes
first

before hipparchus
gains 80
takes

150 tetralogies
opines
lay

Irene Koronas

kera

identity
pure accord iv 58
call xiv 201
the wife of modified
releases the hand
seat of ample
pod queen
confers two anvils
suspend 97
a diadem wide eye

hermes

syncretic creed
in pubic hood

hands
cede plebs

fidelity
on demand

or
by stone finger

filial forms
fed on silt

from snip
and
quick apotheosis

Irene Koronas

erinyes

herself a grotto
deity thong

with menstrual bat heads

burning gnats
and dead cochineal
bees silt any river

pygmalion

Πυγμαλίων
Pumayyaton
fell a statue carve
contents
[hide] external links
depiction ivory
with it
desire
girl lip hard
unparallel workshop
(according to clay anecdote)
simulacrum embrace
the trope inherits
wooden puppets
sentience winter tail
a phonetic refine
otherwise **painting**
miniature literature
undertone sections
die ideal **novel others**
toy sterilization in comic garden
dancing doll echo
shoegazing and darkwave
the plaster body flashlight
reclusive struggles to progress
stage twice cast

crude hole bubblegum
an episode mannequin
in a processing plant
drinking lemon comfort
selling plastic watches
pulled into **interactive fiction**
see also
jump^
jump^
jump^

hesiod 2

[1] absence

oral metric shroud
roots a single span

[2] whom embody greeks
[3] climatic suitors
[4] the hexameter

[5] period
[6] external source
[7][8] two extant sets

vivid long [9] texting
[10] bracket narrative

on in
fact
elegiac
rags remain

[12] eleven lesbos (c 630 c 570 b c)
respect [14] only
[15] additions to monadic

[16] red amphora costume held in full attribute
[17] question
[18] seven

[19] act
[20] three theban centers
[21] nineteen survive reproductions

[23] obscenity comedies
complete [24] poke fun at one
ridicule [25] high skill

[26] satyr popular
[27] bust first half

[28] his book
[29] xenophon 411b c
[30] expel throne praise

[31] philosophy fifth and fourth
accurate least a vague approximation pressed
[32] scholars argue intent
expound own little
figure the same name[33] debate

[34][35] purport to describe his trial
[36] execution

[37] love
[38] and deal
[41] stagira thinkers

[42] first metaphysic desire to know
those who present logic

international [43] million volumes born 295 bc
[44] 13 year epigrams
[45] mimes hint at complete forms
[46] spent [47] influence on 38
[48] mathematics

906 have been lost to measure
the circumference written by archimedes
studied [49] reference frags

[50] [51][52] were probably late

the transition from shift to literary
or rhetorical inclination
all types continue to expand
criticism by hail

[53] saints
[54] probably lived
[55] left off
[56] where
[57] paraphrase or early

[60] bust
[61] a friend in 146 vivid five through 20 parts

[62] from research
[63] consecrate
[64] mentor
[65] publish other essays on [66]
[67] common anecdotes
[68] auto
[69] animalium
[70] (1485) anatomy for the next 1400 years

sketch in 47 volumes [71] 2nd century ad
[72] guides to ruin accuracy

Ptolemy [73] font
[74] a notion
[75] dominate astro
[76] replace
[77] stoics

consider [78] in spite
[79] reform quality
[80] periods
[81] enneads
[82] from compose
[83] dig
[84] fig
[85] second

[86] satirist
[87] faux dialect
[88] novel
[89] transfer [90] [91] as lovers of lies
[92] a version of [93]
[94] unknown [95]

(1912) pp vii kinematic perspective
(1954, 1968) p3 2006 197ff note 64
3836 holds nearer 120 than 150
2011 p309 n29 9780199292011 use (albeit mid and erratic)
2010 p7 9780199803033 (1987) 0-8014-1874-7 (1985)
volume1
(2007) black well universe (1981) from homer to often

Irene Koronas

hesiod 3

(left below)

1 muse
2 cosmogony
3 castration
4 by
5 sea
6 beast
7 the tits
8 hymn
9 cronus
10 prometheus
11 titanomachy
12 raphy
13 us
14 open
15 dress and then

let us mount
broad in thick hold

rod sturdy
they lip her round briny

either side haunts
or lust bolts

[fifty heads strong]

pandora

clays the stole
release

sworn picot
took kylix
to hide in needle

molds gird
and bids breast

rim his knock
up women

drone white comb
bellies two (*pithoi*)
on the (*kakoi*)

those left
siege descent

www.ingramcontent.com/pod-product-compliance
Lightning Source LLC
La Vergne TN
LVHW051604080426
835510LV00020B/3126

* 9 7 8 1 9 1 2 2 1 1 1 3 5 *